READ ONE, READ ALL!

POEMS FOR YOU

READY TO READ THESE AMAZING POEMS?

44 HIGH QUALITY POEMS, GUARANTEED TO ENHANCE YOUR CHILDREN'S VOCABULARY.

FOR AGES 5-13

TABLE OF CONTENTS

I. INTRODUCTION

LIST OF POEMS

A book authored by kids
Enjoyed by Kids and
Especially For kids

THE WORLD OF POEMS

SAGAR.A

HEMRAJ.G

Title: The World of Poems

First Published by Hatchegg Publication in 2022
ISBN: 978-93-90446-12-4
Price in INR: 299/-
www.hatcheggpublication.com
publish@hatcheggpublication.com
+91 8766355652

Cover Design:
Sagar Asani

Distributed by:
Amazon, Flipkart, Manda Publishers etc.

Printer:
Manipal Technologies Ltd.

TABLE OF CONTENTS

LIST OF POEMS

SMILE

How sweet, charming and cute is a smile,
to your profile it adds a bit of style

A smile is a sign to depict happiness,
at times it also describes prettiness

A smile can sometimes beat a charming song,
oh yes it is this strong

God knows why people keep frowning,
instead lets spread a smile to our surrounding

A single smile wins millions of hearts
and its as pure as a block of quartz

To smile or to frown its your choice,
I would prefer a smile its just a piece of advice

CHILDHOOD

There's a time which one enjoys
the time when children annoy

When little minions enjoy and play, every single day
The ones who are innocent and cute and sweet like a kiwi fruit

A phase that never comes back,
when we go to school with a backpack

The time when we get invited to parties where boys get a car and girls Barbies

The time when we break our friendship with children just like our kinship

Lets make our childhood memorable
as we can cherish it in our adulthood

HEALTH

We have often heard that health is wealth
but is it valuable than a bomber's stealth?

Yoga, exercise and meditation
is ideal for regular motion

We all love our health don't we?
we hope its fresh like a tree

In order to maintain a good lifetime
we should have a proper management of time

You all must have learnt the value of health let's
exercise and not be afraid of death

I love my health and you must too
for reading this poem I must thank you

TEACHERS

We often call them second mothers,
that's right they're teachers

They utilize all their energy
in order to improve our memory

As we enter, they smile at us with delight and
lovingly teach us for knowledge is light

Their wisdom makes us successful
and also teaches us not to be stressful

They guide us throughout our school life,
they introduce us to topics and help us dive

So we shall understand their value
and pay them a sweet 'Thank you'

THE MARTYRS

Martyrs day is celebrated in various countries, to pay regards to our honorable armies

Protecting the border and to stop trespassers at the same time the army helps others

Bullets, wars and injury they mostly see,
for their safety there's no guarantee

Their family eagerly waiting for their presence, their kids and wife slowly losing patience

Its because of them we are living safe,
they are really very brave

Salute them and hope their soul rests in peace pray for their family who are seized with grief

FRIENDS

People with whom you can share
everything, from your secrets to the
difficulty of living

With whom you walk, play and talk
everyday, with them you shout 'Hurray'

The ones who make you laugh,
the ones who take you to the right path

The ones who help you make new friends,
the ones who are as valuable as diamonds

The ones on whom we depend,
we hope our friendship never ends

So lets value our friends till they're with
us, else it will be late if we continue
making a fuss

RIVER

How a river flows with pride,
with all its power and might

Ganga, the main river of India,
Niger, the main river of Nigeria

Swag shows the innocent river
it trickles and shines like the luster of
silver

Bathing is a common sight at the river
banks, many people also pay their
thanks

Nowadays people make it dirty
what we don't realize is it's very
worthy

We don't realize the worth of nature's
gift, value the rivers else they may cry
with a click

SPORTS

Cricket, football, tennis are various
sports, played in different types of
courts

Everyone can play sports even who are
small, the best game I love, the best of
all; football

Playing any sport regularly of your
choice,
can help you become swift like a police

One shall learn the value of games
and one must practice it often

By playing sports we can keep
ourselves fit and stop people from
calling us unfit

Games are the best,
it can help us from getting stressed

DOCTORS

They work day and night,
freeing us from our plight

Sorrow, sadness and emotion filled in our mind gets cured by none other than a mastermind

The ones who treats us selflessly
the ones who treats us carefully

An individual or a team,
leaves on our faces a shiny beam

Behind their mask they lie unseen,
who treat everyone from an adult to a teen

This may shock him or her
because this poem is about a doctor

MUSIC

How calm, relaxing it is,
that's right its music

Music can be heard anywhere in nature
it even exists when a pencil scrapes on paper

Imagine life without music,
life would be so basic

Stressful day at work
or difficulty with your homework

Music really helps,
you enjoy and start to yelp

The value of music is not visible to us,
but we may realize it if we look closely
enough

DREAMS

Dreaming is a process that occurs in humans, it can be calm or violent

Some dreams can come true
like you won a car and that too brand new

These may just be a coincidence
I can say that with confidence

Get in a whole new world in your dreams
everything feels so real in your dreams

Jumping from the alps can be dreamt,
but in reality its an impossible event

What ever can be dreamt may not be seen,
like you tomorrow becoming a mighty
queen

GHOSTS

Fear of Darkness, fear of ghosts,
where they exist are places with dusts

Keep your house clean and neat,
else you'll be sorry if a ghost you meet

Shattering windows, Disappearing Feasts
are all signs of fellow ghosts

Fear filled in your mind,
hope the fellow ghost is kind

You might've gotten scared,
once or twice your life may be spared

Well this poem is definitely fake,
else I may never sleep; I'll always stay
awake

EXAMS

Fear of Exams, fear of marks,
eager to know your remarks

We're confused about if we'll pass or fail,
if we pass we'll exclaim; if we fail we'll wail

Why do people cry over marks,
terrified like you're gonna be eaten by a
shark

Why do people take exams too stressfully,
is it cause of them who shout at you severely

Sorrow and sadness filled in your mind,
your friends and family you leave behind

Dear parents forget about the marks please,
a plead from me let their lives stay at ease

SUN

The sun shines high above us,
spreading its heat most on Venus

Without the sun it would be dark all
around, everything would be chilled;
especially towns

Well the light that arrives at night,
is also reflected by the sun with all its might

To us the sun may seem small,
but it is bigger than the biggest mall

The sun is a wonderful source of energy,
it supplies all the light to us generously

Oh how we love you dear sun,
without you we won't have a bit of fun

BIRDS

The ones who soar high in the sky,
with all their power and might they fly

For them the sky is actually the limit,
they fly long distances within a minute

They perch on our windowsill
and glide with all their skill

Asking for more food and water,
especially for their son and daughter

As soon as we keep the food,
they fight over it and suddenly become
rude

I hope I can help these cute birds,
I shall do something now, not afterwards

WATER

Water is a valuable resource,
Lakes, seas and rivers are its main source

Majority of the earth is made of water,
but the earth has less amount of freshwater

We must use water wisely,
there's a lack of water; some get it barely

We shall keep water for our future generations
or else they may suffer dehydration

Water is also important for agriculture,
if we don't leave enough; spoilt will be nature

So let's take a pledge to use water wisely,
else the quantity of water may be really tiny

COPS

The ones who patrol the streets bravely,
the ones who patrol the streets fearlessly

Issuing tickets, catching robbers,
saving millions of dollars

Life at stake, for the community,
they stop robbers usually

They try their best to make the country
safe, stopping people trying to escape

How hard they work in order to stop crime,
the country will be safe and it won't take
time

I salute you officers
because you are very courageous

DOGS

How loyal dogs are, available in many
breeds, they fulfil a man's daily needs.

A dog is known as a man's best friend
and its love towards you will never end

German Shepherd's is a type of breed,
many dogs have various functions and needs

Dogs are the most loyal pets to humans,
by experienced researches it has been proven

They protect us in situations if its light or dark, they save us with their mighty, powerful bark

Lets not shout at them if we have a dog,
cause they'll be with you even when you jog

RAINBOWS

How colorful it is filled with colors of gradient, its worth is even more than a football stadium

Violet, indigo, blue, green, yellow, orange, red it spreads among earth without being tired

This is one of natures most valuable gift,
it appears when the dark clouds lift

It occurs when the sun and droplets meet,
for all of us they give a treat

They disappear too fast,
into the sky that's overcast

What a beautiful gift nature has given us,
we must appreciate it that's a must

COVID-19

Why has this pandemic occurred?
Trillions of rumors we have heard

A horrific virus killing people,
everyone thinks its really evil

To defeat it we must maintain a strong health, and spread the message 'Health is Wealth'

People suffering, Some in need of oxygen,
everyone fearing often

Let's pray for the ones who are infected
let's pray that every one stays protected

Hopefully this virus disappears soon,
else we have to wear a mask even at noon

BEACH

A sunny place best of all,
bouncing a big rubber ball,
not a place like a big hall,
in the beach you can have a long rest.

Watching the waves hit the shore,
relaxes your mind a lot more,
my favorite place is a beach,
and its near distance makes it easy to
reach.

Have fun in the beach,
and enjoy after you reach,
hope you have a fun day at the beach,
eating a delicious small peach.

SCIENTISTS

Scientists work day and night,
to continue the generations of science,

You try experiments and unlock genius things, passion can unlock many amazing things.

If the work is done with interest too,
who knows what you might achieve too?

So, we all hope you feel all right
full of fresh energy to discover more

We all learn from the proof given by you,
you inspire many people including me too

Please continue teaching us more
so like you we all can learn and soar

FATHER

You are joyful and happy,
you love and care,

You are the most loving person I know,
who supports me and helps me grow

You spread your happiness wherever you go, you help me in studies and help me glow

If I ask you something you never say no,
you always tell me everything you know

You work in the office for a long time,
to support the family with love and care,

This awesome person is none other than
my loving, caring, sweet, fascinating
daddy.

EARTH

Green full plants and beautiful skies,
Sunlight hot high in the sky

Sustainable planet with oxygen supplies,
It is you mother earth that we survive

The supporting mother,
our second mother

We cannot survive without our mother
and because we grow crops in its sand

You also provide us with land
and your help is so grand

Many protect and Many hurt,
but still you manage though you're hurt

You are none other than mother earth,
more than everything you are worth

GRANDPARENTS

They look after you as you grow,
and everyday you respect them with a
bow

Always you're happy as can be,
because they help you in a buzz of a bee

When you think of them,
a happy thought floats in your mind

Grandparents are the ones who care for
us with them everything we can discuss

They think of you as the best,
and encourage you to do the rest

They give support and love to you,
its your grandparents who love you too.

BOOKS

or entertainment in free times,
creases vocabulary in time

nteresting adventures you go through
nd enjoy the book as you read through

Vhen you read books time flies,
ut you are not supposed to read it full
ime

time killer it is, but don't read it at night
and of that I am right

Mysteries in nights,
give chills through your spines

When you read you are filled with joy
and you love it because you enjoy

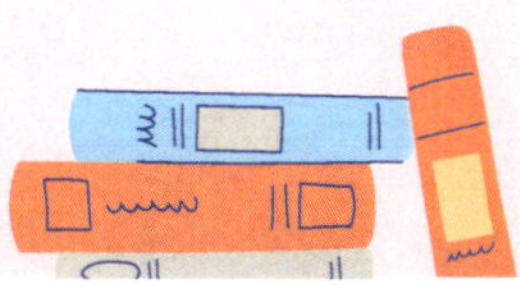

LIFE

You have one chance to live,
one chance to enjoy

Live it with happiness by your side,
life is one humongous ride

With lots of bumps here and there,
we'll have to overcome this ride

Even if there are problems here and there,
happiness is the key to live a good life

Life is a challenge,
life is a gift

Enjoy it to the fullest,
your life will be the purest

FRIENDSHIP

When friends are there,
they're there to help

When you yelp they come to your help.
they shout, enjoy ,they scream, they
laugh

They make you smile,
they make you calm

Its your friends who inspires you more,
and also who helps you score

Thanks for lifting me up,
when I am feeling down

Your friendship means a lot,
this I'd like you to know

OPPORTUNITY

Tough to get,
I can bet

A chance comes once or twice,
not a thousand times

Use it to your best,
and continue the rest

You can get it through a wish,
but it rarely comes and people miss
it

It rarely comes people admit.
opportunities are tough to get

Now that you think about it
isn't it right?

PLANTS

Awesome plants in many types,
giving a lot of oxygen supply

We get food through plants,
so, let's start to keep all plants alive

Without plants we wouldn't survive,
without oxygen and food we'd die

All hail mother earth,
for without her it is impossible to
survive

Plants also have lives,
lets take care of them throughout our
lives

But be careful,
don't feed them rice.

FEELINGS

These things make me cheerful,
sunshine on the beach

Birthday parties, presents,
make me really happy

These things make me sad,
a grey and gloomy day

Unkind words and unkind looks,
when friends just walk away

These things make me angry,
pests who pull my hair

People who break promises
and times when life's not fair

SPRING IS HERE

Spring is here, the snow is gone

What's the green stuff? it's our
lawn

Our coats and hats, we've tossed
aside

Lets grab our bikes,
and take a ride

We will play some catch, and
toss some bees

We will swing some bats, the
day we will seize.

FIRST DAY OF SCHOOL

I wonder if they will be just like me,
or if they will be way better than me

I wonder if they will be friend's with
me, or will I be the lonely kid

I wonder if I will be better than
them,
or if I can run faster than them

I wonder if my teacher ,
will look like mom or gran

I wonder if my puppy will
wonder where I am

WINTER

The sky is dark,
ground is white

The world is peaceful on this windy night. no one around

Not a sound,
to be heard

Not a laugh, not a car,
not even a bird

For a moment,
it's just the snow and me

I smile inside,
I feel so free

RAIN

Rain, rain, drizzling rain,
jumping in puddles when it rains

Rain coat, boots and all,
having fun with a ball

Don't take dolls,
it will get wet

I'll give you a dollar,
for a bet

Jumping around,
here and there

Having fun in the rain,
the rain is insane!

SUMMER

Summer, summer, the heat of summer,
it becomes unbearable

Always sunny; always hot,
I feel like I may rot

Sometimes the sun is warm and cool,
a good time to go to the pool

The heat is not something,
you can fix with a tool

o it is best to swim
a cool pool

ummer is either hot or warm,
d when I am so hot

eel like I am in a,
urning hot pot

HAPPINESS

You cannot buy your happiness, cause
happiness is free

Don't you know, or can't you guess,
it's there for you and me

And what you do,
with what you have got

Can change the way you feel,
just do your best and smile a lot

Cause happiness is made for you, just
take a bite and see

That happiness is what you do,
with something that is free

ANIMALS

Animals do amazing things, and
have amazing habits

Some we like to keep at home,
like cats and dogs and rabbits

Animals live all over the world, in
many kinds of homes

Bats live in caves,
monkeys in trees

And camels in desert zones
hippos live their lives in mud

And polar bears in snow,
kangaroos live on the plains,
where zebra come and go

SLEEP

It's time to recharge your battery,
you wake up with full fresh energy

It's your time to sleep,
get eight hours of good rest

And that day will be your best
refreshed and full with power
is what a sleep will do,

You will be active throughout the
day due to a good night sleep

Sleep on time everyday,
to grow healthy day by day

FESTIVALS

Enjoying day filled with prayers,
like in Holi people spray colors on us

We pray to the lord to ask for his blessings
and sometimes some people sing

Festivals like Diwali is for praying to the lord
and festivals like Holi is to enjoy a lot

We do the daily rituals,
like we do every day

Festivals are the key aspect of our lives,
hopefully festivals last throughout our lives

Make it a habit to thank the lord every day
because all he does for you is unlimited

PARKS

With swings and slides,
and many fun rides

Rollercoaster's with terrifying
heights,
is enough to give shiver through your
spines

Yummy places to eat,
with no unbearable heat

Time to have some fun,
while eating a bun

Place for walking,
place for running

Place for enjoying,
place for gathering

NEIGHBOURS

Let this poem remind you,
that you're special

You're the best neighbour
and the best companion

And so very often too,
you're helpful and supportive

In a way that warms the heart, you're
always here to play your part

Thank you for your kindness,
which can never be repaid

And for your understanding,
and the difference you make

BIRTHDAY

Lots of birthday wishes, lots of birthday smiles

Lots of birthday hugs, lots of birthday miles

Lots of birthday candles, lots of birthday cake

Lots of birthday parties, lots of birthday fun

Lots of birthday vows, lots of birthday lore

Lots of birthday love, and lots more

GOD

Bestows us with blessings,
when asking with sincerity

Helping us, leading us,
when life is going the wrong way

Let's pray for a happy life,
without sadness in our lives

For God is faithful,
his grace will never end

At the lowest, God is my hope,
at my darkest, God is my light

I love God and you should too
because everything he does benefits
you